By Word of Mouth

Selected by
Helen Cook
and
Morag Styles

Illustrated by
Chris Coady

Cambridge University Press

Cambridge
New York   Port Chester
Melbourne   Sydney

Published by the Press Syndicate of the University of Cambridge
The Pitt Building, Trumpington Street, Cambridge CB2 1RP
40 West 20th Street, New York, NY 10011-4211, USA
10 Stamford Road, Oakleigh, Melbourne 3166, Australia

This selection © Cambridge University Press 1991

Illustrations © Chris Coady 1991

Project editor Claire Llewellyn

First published 1991

Printed in Great Britain at the University Press, Cambridge

British Library cataloguing in publication data
By the pricking of my thumbs.
1. Poetry in English – Anthologies
I. Cook, Helen 1954–   II. Styles, Morag
    821.008

ISBN 0 521 39956 4

Acknowledgements

'Applemoon' by Rose Flint from *Writing Poems*, Oxford University Press, reprinted by permission of the author; 'Where Would You Be?' from *Dogs and Dragons, Trees and Dreams* by Karla Kuskin. 'Where Would You Be?' originally appeared in *The Rose on My Cake* by Karla Kuskin. Copyright © 1964 by Karla Kuskin; 'The Hansel and Gretel House' by Gerda Mayer from *The Candyfloss Tree*, Oxford University Press, 1984, reprinted by permission of the author; 'What Was It?' by Kit Wright, from *Cat Among the Pigeons* by Kit Wright (Viking Kestrel, 1987), copyright © Kit Wright, 1987; 'House Fear' from *The Poetry of Robert Frost*, edited by Edward Connery Latham, Jonathan Cape, reprinted by permission of the Estate of Robert Frost, and Henry Holt and Company, Inc. Copyright 1916, © 1969 by Holt, Rinehart and Winston. Copyright 1944 by Robert Frost; 'The Phantom Lollipop Lady' by Adrian Henri from *The Phantom Lollipop Lady* by Adrian Henri, Methuen Children's Books, 1986, copyright © Adrian Henri, 1986; 'The Frozen Man' from *Rabitting On* by Kit Wright, William Collins Sons & Co Ltd, 1978; 'Duppy Dan' from *Black Poetry* published by Blackie 1988, by kind permission of John Agard, c/o Caroline Sheldon Literary Agency; 'The Cunjah Man' by James Edwin Campbell, from *African Poetry for Schools*, East African Publishing House, 1970; 'Why?' from *Jack the Treacle Eater* by Charles Causley, Macmillan, 1987; 'Wolf-Cub Meets the World' by Gareth Owen from *Bright Lights Blaze Out*, Oxford University Press, 1986, by permission of the author; 'Little Fan' © James Reeves from *The Wandering Moon and Other Poems* (Puffin Books) by James Reeves, reprinted by permission of the James Reeves Estate; 'Overheard on a Saltmarsh' by Harold Munro from *The Silent Pool*, by permission of Duckworth; 'Water Sprite' by Miroslav Holub translated by Ian Milner from *Selected Poems: Miroslav Holub* (Penguin Books, 1967), © Penguin Books, 1967, reproduced by permission of Penguin Books.

Every effort has been made to reach copyright holders; the publishers would be glad to hear from anyone whose rights they have unknowingly infringed.

Contents

Witches and Wizards   5
Anon

EXTRACT FROM Macbeth   5
William Shakespeare

Charm   6
Ben Jonson

Omens   7
Traditional, Gaelic

Applemoon   8
Rose Flint

Where Would You Be?   10
Karla Kuskin

The Hansel and Gretel House   11
Gerda Mayer

What Was It?   12
Kit Wright

House Fear   13
Robert Frost

The Phantom Lollipop Lady   14
Adrian Henri

The Frozen Man   16
Kit Wright

Duppy Dan   18
John Agard

Phantom *Samuel Taylor Coleridge*	19
A Spell to Destroy Life *Cherokee, Native American*	20
La Belle Dame Sans Merci *John Keats*	22
The Cunjah Man *James Edwin Campbell*	24
Why? *Charles Causley*	26
Wolf-Cub Meets the World *Gareth Owen*	28
Little Fan *James Reeves*	30
Overheard on a Saltmarsh *Harold Munro*	31
Water Sprite *Miroslav Holub*	32

Witches and Wizards

From witches and wizards and
   longtail'd buzzards
And creeping things that run
   in hedge bottoms,
Good Lord deliver us.

                Anon

EXTRACT FROM Macbeth

Light thickens, and the crow
makes wing to the rooky wood;
Good things of the day begin to droop and drowse,
Whiles night's black agents to their preys do rouse!

                William Shakespeare

Charm

The owl is abroad, the bat and the toad,
    And so is that cat-a-mountain,
The ant, and the mole fit both in a hole,
    The frog peeps out of the fountain;
The dogs, they do bay, and the timbrels play
    The spindle is now a-turning;
The moon it is red, and the stars are fled,
    But all the sky is a-burning.

Ben Jonson

Omens

I heard the cuckoo with no food in my stomach,
I heard the stock-dove on the top of the tree,
I heard the sweet singer in the copse beyond,
And I heard the screech of the owl of the night.

I saw the lamb with his back to me,
I saw the snail on the bare flag-stone,
I saw the foal with his rump to me,
I saw the snipe while sitting bent,
And I foresaw that the year would not
   Go well with me.

Traditional, Gaelic

Applemoon

Something woke me: startle-sound
or moonlight. The house dreamt
like an old cat, but I
looked out my window.

And night was day in a midnight
moon-flood. Mazy moon
flaring a halo of quick clouds
running the big black sky.
And I saw a thousand windfall apples
lying luminous as sea-stones beached
below the spiky silver trees.

So, shivering I
mouse-went out
with a basket, barefoot, toes
curling in the cold;
and singing soft
took ripe reluctant apples
under close and curious stars.

Only soon I saw
my shadow was not
the same as I;
it stooped more –
had its own thinness . . .
and our fingers
never met.

I quick-ran back
the house so
sleepy-warm, sure.
But looking out through curtain lace
I saw my shadow linger
moving slow and crooked, plucking
shadow apples
from the shining moony grass.

Rose Flint

Where Would You Be?

Where would you be on a night like this
With the wind so dark and howling?
Close to the light
Wrapped warm and tight
Or where the cats are prowling?

Where would you wish you on such a night
Where the twisting trees are tossed?
Safe in a chair
In the lamp-lit air
Or out where the moon is lost?

Where would you be when the white waves roar
On the tumbling storm-torn sea?
Tucked inside
Where it's calm and dry
Or searching for stars in a furious sky
Whipped by the whine of the Gale's wild cry
Out in the Night with me?

Karla Kuskin

The Hansel and Gretel House

When you come across it
you'll know better than to
nibble.
Who's there? asks the witch.
The wind, cry the
startled children.

A house may look sweet
from outside: beware!
Things happen in pretty houses
you wouldn't believe . . .

When the wind cries,
when the dog weeps,
when the voice of lost children
is heard in the wood,
let the forester hasten forth.

Gerda Mayer

What Was It?

What was it
that could make
me wake
in the middle of the night
when the light
was a long way from coming
and the humming
of the fridge was the single
tingle
of sound
all round?

Why, when I crept downstairs and watched
green numbers sprinting on the kitchen clock,
was I afraid the empty rocking chair
might start to rock?

Why, when I stole back up and heard
the creak of each stair to my own
heart's quickening beats,

was I afraid that I should find
some other thing from the night outside
between my sheets?

Kit Wright

House Fear

Always – I tell you this they learned –
Always at night when they returned
To the lonely house from far away
To lamps unlighted and fire gone grey,
They learned to rattle the lock and key
To give whatever might chance to be
Warning and time to be off in flight:
And preferring the out- to the in-door night,
They learned to leave the house-door wide
Until they had lit the lamp inside.

Robert Frost

The Phantom Lollipop Lady

The phantom lollipop lady
haunts the crossroads
where the old school used to be;
they closed it down in 1973.

The old lollipop lady
loved her job, and stood there
for seven years altogether,
no matter how bad the weather.

When they pulled the old school down
she still stood there every day:
a pocketful of sweets for the little ones,
smiles and a joke for the big ones.

One day the lollipop lady
was taken away to hospital.
Without her standing there
the corner looked, somehow, bare.

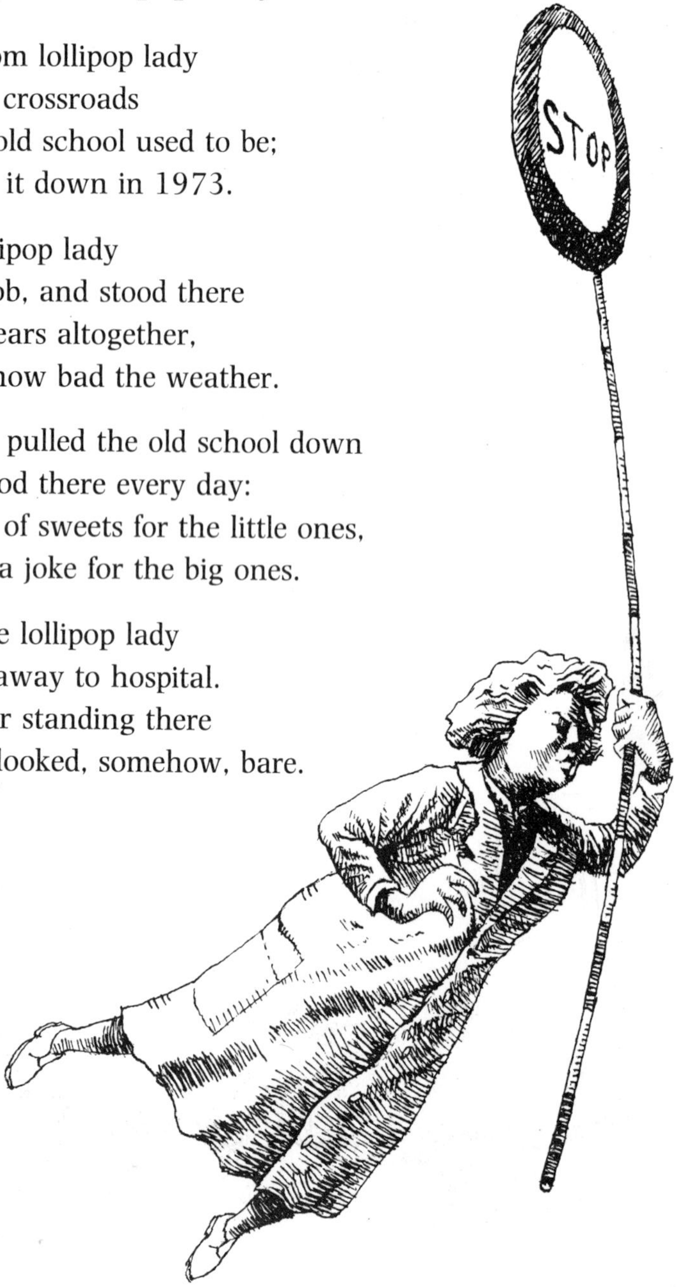

After a month and two operations
the lollipop lady died;
the children felt something missing:
she had made her final crossing.

Now if you go down alone at dusk
just before the streetlights go on,
look closely at the corner over there:
in the shadows by the lamp-post you'll see her.

Helping phantom children across the street,
holding up the traffic with a ghostly hand;
at the twilight crossing where four roads meet
the phantom lollipop lady stands.

Adrian Henri

The Frozen Man

Out at the edge of town
where black trees

crack their fingers
in the icy wind

and hedges freeze
on their shadows

and the breath of cattle,
still as boulders,

hangs in rags
under the rolling moon,

a man is walking
alone:

on the coal-black road
his cold

feet
ring

and
ring.

Here in a snug house
at the heart of town

the fire is burning
red and yellow and gold:

you can hear the warmth
like a sleeping cat

breathe softly
in every room.

When the frozen man
comes to the door,

let him in,
let him in,
let him in.

Kit Wright

Duppy Dan

Duppy Dan
aint no livin man

Duppy Dan
done dead an gone

Duppy Dan
nah have foot

Duppy Dan
nah have hand

Yet Duppy Dan cross water
Duppy Dan cross land

Duppy Dan ride white horse
pon pitchdark night

Run like-a-hell stranger
when Duppy Dan tell you goodnight

John Agard

Phantom

All look and likeness caught from earth,
All accident of kin and birth,
Had pass'd away. There was no trace
Of aught on that illumined face,
Uprais'd beneath the rifted stone
But of one spirit all her own; –
She, she herself, and only she,
Shone thro' her body visibly.

Samuel Taylor Coleridge

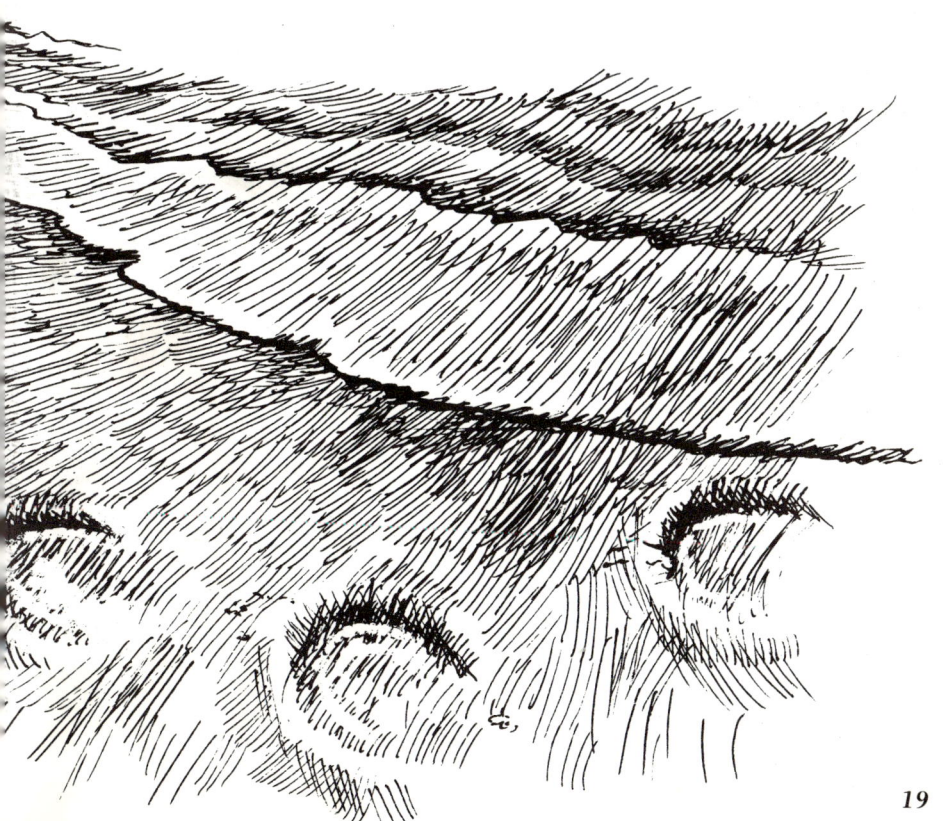

A Spell to Destroy Life

Listen!
   Now I have come to step over your soul
     (I know your clan)
     (I know your name)
     (I have stolen your spit and buried it under earth)
   I bury your soul under earth
   I cover you over with black rock
   I cover you over with black cloth
   I cover you over with black slabs
   You disappear forever

   Your path leads to the
     Black Coffin
      in the hills of the Darkening Land

  So let it be for you

   The clay of the hills covers you
   The black clay of the Darkening Land

  Your soul fades away

   It becomes blue (colour of despair)
   When darkness comes your spirit shrivels and
     dwindles to disappear forever
Listen!

                  Cherokee, Native American

La Belle Dame Sans Merci

O, what can ail thee, knight-at-arms,
    Alone and palely loitering?
The sedge has wither'd from the lake,
    And no birds sing.

O, what can ail thee, knight-at-arms,
    So haggard and so woe-begone?
The squirrel's granary is full,
    And the harvest's done.

I see a lilly on thy brow,
    With anguish moist and fever dew;
And on thy cheeks a fading rose
    Fast withereth too.

I met a lady in the meads,
    Full beautiful – a faery's child,
Her hair was long, her foot was light,
    And her eyes were wild.

I made a garland for her head,
    And bracelets too, and fragrant zone;
She look'd at me as she did love,
    And made sweet moan.

I set her on my pacing steed,
    And nothing else saw all day long;
For sidelong would she bend, and sing
    A faery's song.

She found me roots of relish sweet,
   And honey wild, and manna dew,
And sure in language strange she said –
   'I love thee true'.

She took me to her elfin grot,
   And there she wept and sigh'd full sore,
And there I shut her wild wild eyes
   With kisses four.

And there she lulled me asleep
   And there I dream'd – Ah! woe betide!
The latest dream I ever dream'd
   On the cold hill's side.

I saw pale knights and princes too,
   Pale warriors, death-pale were they all:
They cried – 'La Belle Dame sans Merci
   Hath thee in thrall!'

I saw their starved lips in the gloam
   With horrid warning gaped wide,
And I awoke and found me here
   On the cold hill's side.

And this is why I sojourn here
   Alone and palely loitering,
Though the sedge is wither'd from the lake,
   And no birds sing.

John Keats

The Cunjah Man

O children, run, the Cunjah Man,
Him mouth as big as frying-pan,
Him ears am small, him eyes am red,
Him have no tooth in him old head,
Him have him roots, him work him trick,
Him roll him eye, him make you sick –
   The Cunjah Man, the Cunjah Man,
   O children, run, the Cunjah Man!

Him have a ball of red, red hair,
Him hide it under the kitchen stair,
Mam Jude, her pass along that way,
And now her have a snake, they say.
Him wrap around her body tight,
Her eyes pop out, a awful sight –
   The Cunjah Man, the Cunjah Man,
   O children, run, the Cunjah Man!

Miss Jane, her drive him from her door,
And now her hens won't lay no more;
The Jersey cow, her done fall sick,
It's all done by the Cunjah trick.
Him put a root under 'Lijah's bed,
And now the man, he sure am dead –
    The Cunjah Man, the Cunjah Man,
    O children, run, the Cunjah Man!

Me see him stand the other night,
Right in the road in white moon-light;
Him toss him arms, him whirl him round,
Him stomp him foot upon the ground;
The snakes come crawling, one by one,
Me hear them hiss, me break and run –
    The Cunjah Man, the Cunjah Man,
    O children, run, the Cunjah Man!

James Edwin Campbell

Why?

Why do you turn your head, Susanna,
And why do you swim your eye?
It's only the children on Bellman Street
Calling, *A Penny for the guy!*

Why do you look away, Susanna,
As the children wheel him by?
It's only a dummy in an old top-hat
And a fancy jacket and tie.

Why do you take my hand, Susanna,
As the pointing flames jump high?
It's only a bundle of sacking and straw.
Nobody's going to die.

Why is your cheek so pale, Susanna,
As the whizzbangs flash and fly?
It's nothing but a rummage of paper and rag
Strapped to a stick you spy.

Why do you say you hear, Susanna,
The sound of a last, long sigh?
And why do you say it won't leave your head
No matter how hard you try?

Best let me take you home, Susanna.
Best on your bed to lie.
It's only a dummy in an old top-hat.
Nobody's going to die.

Charles Causley

Wolf-Cub Meets the World

What is that howling, my mother,
Howling out of the sky
That rustles the branches and bends the pines
And throws the cold snow in my eye?

>That is the wind, my wolf son,
>The breath of the world passing by
>That flattens the grasses and whips up the lake
>And hurls clouds and birds through the sky.

What is that eye gleaming red, mother,
Gleaming red in the face of the sky?
Why does it stare at me so, mother,
Why does its fire burn my eye?

>That is the sun, my wolf child,
>That changes dark night into day
>That warms your grey fur and the pine-needled floor
>And melts the cold snow away.

And who is that serpent that glides, mother,
And winds the dark rocks among;
Who laughs and sings as he slides through my paws
And tastes so cold on my tongue?

    That is the river, my curious son,
    That no creature alive can outrun.
    He cuts out the valleys and makes watery lakes
    And was here when the world first began.

And whose is the face that I see, mother,
That face in the water so clear?
Why when I try to touch him
Does he always disappear?

Gareth Owen

Little Fan

'I don't like the look of little Fan, mother,
    I don't like her looks a little bit.
Her face – well, it's not exactly different,
    But there's something wrong with it.

'She went down to the sea-shore yesterday,
    And she talked to somebody there.
Now she won't do anything but sit
    And comb out her yellowy hair.

'Her eyes are shiny and she sings, mother,
    Like nobody ever sang before.
Perhaps they gave her something queer to eat,
    Down by the rocks on the shore.

'Speak to me, speak, little Fan dear,
    Aren't you feeling very well?
Where have you been and what are you singing,
    And what's that seaweedy smell?

'Where did you get that shiny comb, love,
    And those pretty coral beads so red?
Yesterday you had two legs, I'm certain,
    But now there's something else instead.

'I don't like the looks of little Fan, mother,
    You'd best go and close the door.
Watch now, or she'll be gone for ever
    To the rocks by the brown sandy shore.'

James Reeves

Overheard on a Saltmarsh

Nymph, nymph, what are your beads?

Green glass, goblin. Why do you stare at them?

Give them me.

    No.

Give them me. Give them me.

    No.

Then I will howl all night in the reeds,
Lie in the mud and howl for them.

Goblin, why do you love them so?

They are better than stars or water,
Better than voices of winds that sing,
Better than any man's fair daughter,
Your green glass beads on a silver ring.

Hush, I stole them out of the moon.

Give me your beads, I want them.

    No.

I will howl in a deep lagoon
For your green glass beads, I love them so.
Give them me. Give them me.

    No.

Harold Munro

Water Sprite

You just have to
    start blowing bubbles underwater from the crack of dawn,
    stir up ripples all the morning,
    at noontime run the water off your coat-tails on the
        strips between the fields,
    all afternoon tread the wind in wavy ridges,
    at dusk start croaking at the moon, –

no one has the time today
just to sit and do a little haunting.

Miroslav Holub